# ZEN STORIES

## The Monkey,
## the Cat & the Lotus

58 Mind–Opening Teachings of Wisdom to Help You
Find Lasting Peace

Han Ching

# CONTENTS

AUTHOR'S NOTE    6

SIX-WINDOW MONKEY    7

A ZEN CAT'S WAY    8

LOTUS IN THE MUD    9

MONK AND NIGHTINGALE    11

HIDDEN EMBER    13

CICADA'S SHELL    15

SCHOLAR'S NAME    16

GARDENER'S WISDOM    18

FERRYMAN'S LAST LESSON    20

WATER BOWL TEACHING    23

FORBIDDEN VEGETABLE    25

PLAYFUL MASTER    26

MIND LIKE A MIRROR    28

ORANGE AND THE SUN    30

SOUND OF SLEEP    32

MASTER OF STILLNESS    33

HIDDEN THIEF    35

STONE IN THE SNOW    37

COLORS OF PURITY    39

CIRCLE IN THE AIR    40

A QUESTION OF DONKEYS    42

DHARMA IN A PINCH    44

MOUNTAIN'S SECRET    45

GOOSE IN THE BOTTLE    46

WRONG READING, RIGHT AWAKENING    47

MENDER OF EMPTY SPACE    49

DANCING WITH CATTLE    51

FLOWER IN THE INCENSE BURNER    52

ANCIENT BUDDHA IN THE KITCHEN    53

WOOD CARRIER'S ENLIGHTENMENT    55

SIX ONES    57

SLEEPING SAGE    58

GARDEN OF NO SHADOWS    60

PORTRAIT'S SECRET    62

FIRE TONGS    64

MUTE'S HONEY    66

SNOWY DIALOGUE    67

ILLITERATE SAGE    68

YESTERDAY'S RAIN, TODAY'S SUN    70

WATCH THE FIRE!    72

IMAGINARY DOG    73

THREE PHRASES 74

POETRY TRAP 75

MOUNTAIN PATH 77

MASTER OF TIME 78

BAMBOO SIEVE MAKERS 79

BURNING STATUE 81

CANDLE 82

SIMPLE WAY 83

HEART'S MIRROR 84

BEYOND FORMALITIES 85

WITHOUT WORDS 86

ONE LETTER 87

WANDERER 88

TWO TRUTHS 89

LOCK WITHOUT A DOOR 90

BURNED EYEBROWS 91

SILENT DANCE OF TWO MOUNTAINS 93

# AUTHOR'S NOTE

The stories in this book are like fallen leaves, scattered and forgotten by time. I have gathered them gently, letting their light glimmer once more.

These are not lessons to be learned or truths to be grasped. They are reflections—silent and clear—for you to simply see.

Do not search for meaning. Let the words settle, like ripples in a still pond. In their quiet, they may reveal what has always been here.

What you seek has never been lost.

# SIX-WINDOW MONKEY

A young seeker approached a master with a question that had long puzzled him. "What is the nature of Buddha-mind?" he asked.

The master smiled and replied, "Let me tell you a story. Imagine a room with six windows, and inside is a monkey. Outside, other monkeys call to it. When they call from the east window, 'Hey!' the monkey inside responds. The same happens at all six windows—every call receives a response."

The seeker bowed respectfully and said, "Thank you for this teaching, but I have one doubt."

"What troubles you?" the master asked.

"What happens when the monkey inside is sleeping, and the monkey outside wishes to meet it?"

The master rose from his meditation seat, gently took the seeker's hand, and said softly, "Look—the monkey has already met you."

~~~~~~~~~~

The six senses—eyes, ears, nose, tongue, body, and mind—are like different doorways, yet they all arise from the same heart. The monkey rushing between six windows—isn't this just like us? Tossing between joy and anger, struggling amidst gain and loss?

# A ZEN CAT'S WAY

One autumn morning, a cat wandered into the meditation hall and sat down next to the master. A young monk, new to the temple, frowned at this disturbance.

"Master," he whispered, "shouldn't we chase away this cat? It's disrupting our practice."

The master opened his eyes and gazed at the cat, which sat perfectly still, its breath rising and falling like gentle waves.

"If it comes, it sits in meditation. If it goes, it goes. It follows its nature perfectly. What could be more enlightened than that?"

The young monk looked at the cat again, and for the first time, he saw not a distraction, but a teacher.

～～～～～～～

What comes, comes. What goes, goes. The cat knows this without knowing.

# LOTUS IN THE MUD

In those days, farmers were considered the lowest class, forbidden even to enter temples as monks. Yet there was one who yearned so deeply for the Buddhist path that he concealed his background, taking on a noble family name to fulfill his dream.

Years passed, and his wisdom and compassion earned him such respect that he was chosen to become the head abbot. On the day of the inauguration ceremony, as incense smoke curled through the great hall and hundreds gathered to witness the sacred moment, a voice suddenly cut through the solemn atmosphere.

"How dare you!" A figure emerged from the crowd—a merchant who had knowledge of the abbot's past. Pointing an accusing finger toward the platform, the merchant shouted, "A farmer's child sitting on the abbot's seat? Have you all lost your minds?"

The hall fell into deadly silence. The drum stopped. No one dared breathe, let alone speak. Even the temple bells seemed to hold their tone.

All eyes turned to the new abbot, waiting to see how he would handle this revelation. But there was no trace of shame or fear on his face. Instead, a serene smile played across his lips as he spoke just three words:

"Lotus in mud."

The simple phrase hung in the air like temple incense. Then, understanding dawned on every face, followed by murmurs of appreciation that grew into thunderous approval. Even the accuser stood speechless.

The ceremony continued, and from that day, the abbot's wisdom was revered even more deeply than before.

~~~~~~~~~~

We often believe our origins define our destiny, yet the lotus teaches us otherwise. Rising from the darkest mud, it blooms unstained. Our true nature doesn't depend on where we began, but on how we bloom in this moment.

# MONK AND NIGHTINGALE

In a remote mountain temple, there lived a humble monk. Day after day, he devoted himself to studying the Lotus Sutra, seeking its deepest wisdom. One passage in particular caught in his mind like a thorn:

"All phenomena, from their very origin, manifest the nature of stillness and extinction."

These words puzzled him deeply. He carried the question with him through every moment of his daily life—while sweeping the temple grounds, during meditation, even as he lay down to sleep. The meaning was elusive, like trying to grasp the wind or catch the moon's reflection in water.

One spring evening, as he sat in his simple quarters with moonlight streaming through the paper windows, the monk was once again immersed in this eternal riddle. The night was silent, the air fresh with spring's gentle touch. Suddenly, a nightingale's clear song broke through the quiet.

In that crystalline moment, as the bird's song merged with the moonlight and the stillness of the spring night, everything fell into place. The monk's confusion dissolved like morning mist under the rising sun. He finally understood: the truth had been present all along, in every moment, in every breath.

With joy in his heart, he completed the verse:

"All phenomena, from their very origin,

Manifest the nature of stillness and extinction.
When spring arrives, a hundred flowers bloom,
And the nightingale sings in the willow tree."

~~~~~~~~~~~

Just as moonlight needs no explanation to illuminate the night, the deepest truths reveal themselves in life's simplest moments.

# HIDDEN EMBER

In a mountain temple where winter winds whispered through ancient pines, a master sat in his quiet quarters one evening. A student stood nearby, attending to the teacher as shadows danced on the walls.

"Who's there?" the master asked, though he already knew who was present.

"It is I, your student," came the reply.

"Check if there are any embers left in the brazier," the master instructed.

The student stirred the ashes briefly and responded, "No fire remains."

The master rose slowly, took up the fire tongs, and reached deep into the ashes. With careful probing, he uncovered a tiny, glowing ember. Lifting it up, he showed it to the student and asked, "Then what do you call this?"

In that moment, as the small ember cast its gentle light, something awakened in the student's mind. He bowed deeply.

The master nodded and spoke softly: "This is but a temporary divergence on your path. The sutras tell us that to understand Buddha-nature, we must observe the moments and conditions. When the time is right, confusion becomes clarity, like suddenly remembering what was forgotten. What we seek has always been our own possession. After awakening, it's just as before—no mind, no dharma, only the absence of delusion and the dropping away of ordinary and sacred distinctions. Your original nature has always been complete. Now that you see this, guard it well."

The next day, as master and student worked together on the mountainside, the master asked, "Did you bring the fire?"

"Yes, I did," the student replied.

"Where is it?"

The student picked up a branch, blew on it twice, and handed it to the master.

The master smiled and said, "Like an insect boring through wood—marks appear without intention."

~~~~~~~~~~~~~~

How often do we declare, "There is nothing," when we have only scratched the surface? The ember of truth glows eternal, whether we see it or not.

# CICADA'S SHELL

On a warm summer day, a master and his attendant wandered along a mountain path. Sunlight filtered through the leaves, creating dancing shadows on the ground. As they walked, the master's eyes caught sight of something translucent clinging to a tree branch.

It was an empty cicada shell, delicate and perfectly preserved, still hanging where its former inhabitant had emerged.

The attendant, noticing it too, asked thoughtfully, "Master, the shell remains here, but where has the cicada gone?"

The master didn't speak. Instead, he gently picked up the empty shell and held it to his ear. With playful wisdom in his eyes, he shook it softly three times, and then, unexpectedly, made the sound of a cicada's song: Tsssssssss...

In that moment, all the attendant's questions about coming and going, about life and death, about presence and absence—dissolved in the simple clarity of the moment.

~~~~~~~~~~~

*We search endlessly for what cannot be lost. The cicada's song echoes everywhere—in the shell, in the trees, in the silence. Who is listening? When we stop seeking the cicada beyond its shell, we might hear its eternal song within ourselves.*

# SCHOLAR'S NAME

In the misty mountains of ancient times, a scholar approached the monastery of a renowned master. Though known for his cleverness, he humbly introduced himself as "the Clumsy One."

The master, seated in his simple quarters, looked at him and asked, "What is your name?"

"My surname is Chang, and I am called Cho, meaning 'Clumsy,'" the scholar replied.

The master's eyes sparkled as he responded, "If even skillfulness cannot be found, from where does clumsiness come?"

In that moment, understanding came effortlessly, and the scholar began to compose these verses:

Radiant wisdom illuminates countless worlds,
All beings, sacred and ordinary, share my home.
When not a single thought arises, reality shines complete,
Yet when the senses stir, clouds obscure the light.
To cut off troubles only breeds more illness,
Even pursuing truth becomes a crooked path.
Following life's flow without resistance,
Nirvana and birth-death are both empty flowers.

The master nodded in recognition, seeing that the scholar had penetrated the heart of the matter. The one who came seeking wisdom had found what they didn't know they already possessed.

Names and labels—skillful or clumsy, wise or foolish—are like clouds passing through the sky. When we stop grasping at them, what remains? The nameless reality that was always here, as natural as breathing.

# GARDENER'S WISDOM

In a mountain monastery, a young monk approached the master to bid farewell, seeking to continue his spiritual journey elsewhere.

"Mountains surround us on all sides," the master said. "Where will you go?"

The monk stood silent, his mind blank as fresh snow.

"You have ten days," the master declared. "Find the right words, and you may leave."

Day after day, the troubled monk wandered the monastery grounds like a restless ghost, his mind churning with possible answers. His feet eventually carried him to the vegetable garden, where the head gardener was quietly tending to the plants.

Noticing the monk's distress, the gardener asked, "If you wish to leave, why do you linger here?"

After hearing the monk's predicament, the gardener smiled and spoke softly:

Dense bamboo cannot stop flowing water,

High mountains cannot block drifting clouds.

The monk's face lit up with joy. The gardener added quietly, "But do not say these words came from me."

When the monk presented these words to the master, the master's eyes narrowed. "Whose words are these?"

"They are mine," the monk claimed.

"No," the master replied, "they are not."

Seeing he could not deceive the master, the monk

confessed that the words had come from the gardener.

That evening, the master gathered the assembly and announced, "Do not underestimate our gardener. One day, five hundred students will sit at his feet."

Years later, the gardener returned to his hometown and established a temple on Cloud Dwelling Mountain. Just as the master had foreseen, over five hundred disciples gathered to learn from the one who had once quietly tended vegetables in the monastery.

~~~~~~~~~~~~~~

*Dense bamboo cannot stop flowing water, high mountains cannot block drifting clouds - Who is truly confined?*

# FERRYMAN'S LAST LESSON

In the misty waters where rivers met, an unusual monk spent thirty years operating a small ferry. Few suspected that this simple ferryman was a deeply enlightened teacher who had chosen this humble life. Before leaving his monastery years ago, the monk had said:

"I love only mountains and waters. Here I will wait by the river for one worthy student to whom I can pass on our teaching."

And so he waited, day after day, year after year, known simply as "the Boat Monk" to travelers who crossed his ferry.

In a nearby city, a monk known for his scholarship was giving Buddhist lectures. Though learned in scriptures, something was missing from his understanding. During one of his talks, another monk asked him about the nature of reality:

"What is the dharma body?"

"The dharma body has no form," the scholarly monk replied confidently.

"What is the dharma eye?"

"The dharma eye has no flaw."

Among the listeners was a master who knew the ferryman well. Hearing these answers, the master couldn't help but laugh. After the talk, the scholarly monk approached him with humble curiosity:

"Why did you laugh at my answers?"

"You speak from books, not experience," the master replied kindly. "There's someone you should meet—the Boat Monk. But leave your scholarly robes behind when you go."

Following this advice, the scholarly monk changed into simple clothes and sought out the ferryman. Their first meeting sparked an unusual dialogue:

"Where do you reside?" asked the ferryman.

"Beyond any fixed place," replied the scholarly monk.

"And what brings you here?"

"I seek understanding beyond mere appearances."

The ferryman's eyes sparkled with interest. He posed a challenge:

"The fishing line hangs deep in still waters. Three inches from the hook—speak the truth!"

As the scholarly monk opened his mouth to give a clever answer, the ferryman suddenly struck him with his oar, sending him splashing into the river. As the monk grabbed the boat's edge, gasping, the ferryman called out:

"Speak now! Not from your knowledge, but from your heart!"

Again, the scholarly monk tried to answer, and again he was struck. But this time, something profound shifted within him. Drenched and breathless, he experienced a moment of pure clarity. He looked up at the ferryman and nodded three times, words no longer necessary.

The old ferryman smiled. "Now you understand. The truth is like playing with a fishing line—the game is not in catching thoughts, but in dancing with reality itself."

Before they parted, the ferryman gave one last teaching:

"When you teach others, hide yourself where there are traces, and leave traces where you hide. Seek the deep mountains, find one or two worthy students, and keep our lineage alive."

As the scholarly monk walked away, he couldn't help glancing back several times. Seeing this lingering doubt, the old master called out one final time. When the scholar turned, the ferryman stood in his boat, oar raised high:

"Do you still think there's something more to understand?"

Then, with a sudden movement, he capsized his boat and vanished beneath the waters, leaving only ripples that slowly faded into the smooth surface of the river.

~~~~~~~~~~~~~

True teaching often comes not through words, but through direct experience. The ferryman waited thirty years to find one worthy student, then disappeared like ripples on water, leaving only the essence of his teaching behind.

# WATER BOWL TEACHING

In ancient times, a young monk served as an attendant to a renowned Zen master. One summer day, master and student went into the mountains to cut wood. During their rest, the master handed the student a bowl of water. The student drank it without hesitation.

"Do you understand?" the master asked.

"No, I don't," the student replied honestly.

The master handed him another bowl of water. Again, the student drank it.

"Do you understand now?" the master asked again.

"No, I still don't," the student answered.

The master leaned forward and said, "Why don't you investigate this 'not understanding' itself?"

The student tilted his head and replied, "If I don't understand, what is there to investigate?"

The master smiled. "You're like an iron stake—unmovable!"

At these words, the student bowed deeply, having glimpsed something essential.

Years later, after the student had become a master and established his own temple, his senior dharma brother came to visit. Over tea, the elder monk brought up that day in the mountains.

"The master approved of me then," the younger master said with pride.

"Ah," the elder monk replied, "you left your teacher

too soon."

A bowl of water sat between them. The elder monk pointed to it. "Pass me the water."

When the younger master handed him the bowl, the elder monk simply poured it out.

In that moment, the younger master's final attachment—to the very idea of understanding and approval—dissolved completely, like water returning to the earth.

~~~~~~~~~

Sometimes the wisest stance is to simply say, "I don't know," and remain there, honest and unmoved. Like an iron stake planted in the earth, this pure presence is more real than any understanding we might chase.

# FORBIDDEN VEGETABLE

A master tended the monastery garden one morning. He drew a circle in the dirt around a single bok choy and told his students, "No one touch this."

The students nodded solemnly and stayed clear of the circle.

Later that day, the master returned. The garden had been harvested for the evening meal - carrots pulled, greens gathered. Only his circled bok choy stood pristine and untouched in its ring of dust. Laughing like thunder, he grabbed his staff and chased every student from the garden.

"Not a single one of you knows true wisdom!"

~~~~~~~~~~~~~~~~

A circle in the dirt becomes a prison of obedience. When following rules perfectly becomes its own barrier, who dares to pick the vegetable of wisdom?

# PLAYFUL MASTER

A Zen master was known for his lively and witty way of teaching. Here are four encounters that reveal his unique approach:

## THE NAME GAME

One day, a monk came to visit.

"What's your name?" asked the master.

"My name means 'Teaching of Light,'" replied the monk.

"Do you understand teaching, then?"

"To some extent," the monk answered.

"At the sacred assembly on Vulture Peak, where the Buddha taught his disciples," the master said while raising his fist, "what would you call this?"

"The teaching of the fist," the monk replied cleverly, making a pun between 'fist' and 'authority.'

"If that's so..." the master laughed, then stretched out his feet. "What teaching is this?"

The monk was silent.

"Why not call it the teaching of feet?" the master teased.

## THE TIGER'S DEN

Another monk asked, "What if there's a thousand-foot cliff in front and tigers behind?"

"Be free," the master answered simply.

## THE REAL MASTER

"Who is the master of all realms?" a monk asked, seeking profound philosophical insight.

The master replied with striking simplicity: "Can you eat your food?"

## THE FINAL TEACHING

On his last day, the master gathered his students. Many expected a profound teaching. The master remained silent, then extended his left hand and instructed those on the east side to step back. He extended his right hand and asked those on the west side to do the same.

Finally, he spoke: "To repay the Buddha's kindness, nothing surpasses spreading the great teaching. I'm going home! I'm going home! Take care!" With a gentle smile, he passed away.

~~~~~~~~~~~~~~~~

Each moment is the perfect teaching - a fist, a foot, a meal, a smile. The master showed us that Zen lives not in grand philosophies but in life itself, played out with joy.

# MIND LIKE A MIRROR

A young monk sought solitude in the northern mountains, where ice-covered peaks sparkled like crystal under the winter sun. His small hut stood near a wooden bridge spanning a rushing stream. At first, the sounds of nature overwhelmed him—the howling wind through ancient pines, the water crashing over rocks, the endless symphony of the mountain.

"I cannot meditate," he confessed to his teacher before the elder departed. "The sounds are too loud."

The teacher smiled gently. "The sounds arise from your mind, not from outside. Remember the ancient saying: one who listens to the water for thirty years without turning from its sound will understand true hearing."

Taking these words to heart, the monk began sitting on the narrow wooden bridge each day. Below him, the stream sang its endless song. At first, the sound filled his ears like thunder. Gradually, he noticed that the water's voice only appeared when his thoughts reached for it.

Days turned into months. The monk lived simply, making thin porridge from wheat husks and wild vegetables. A small bag of rice lasted him half a year.

One day, while walking his usual path, the monk stopped. In that moment, his body and mind dropped away. All that remained was vast brightness, perfectly still, like a great mirror reflecting mountains and rivers. When awareness of his body returned, he couldn't say how long he had stood there. Returning to his hut, he found white mold covering his cooking pot.

He wrote:

When the wild mind suddenly stills,
Inner and outer worlds become crystal clear.
Turning around, I break through empty space—
All things arise and fade in perfect time.

From that day forward, sounds no longer disturbed his peace. The mountain's song had become his own silence.

~~~~~~~~~~~

When the mind becomes like a clear mirror, both sound and silence dance on its surface, leaving no trace.

# ORANGE AND THE SUN

In a quiet mountain monastery, a young monk arrived to begin his training. Being new, he was first assigned to help in the guest quarters, performing daily tasks such as distributing oranges to the other monks.

One morning, during his duties, someone asked him, "Where have you come from?"

"From beyond the mountains," the young monk replied.

"Such a long journey must have been tiring," remarked the other monk.

The young monk simply held up an orange and said, "Orange! Orange!"

Later that day, he went to meet the head of the monastery for the first time. As the monks gathered in the great hall, the young monk approached the master's seat. Their eyes met in a single, profound glance. Then, without saying a word, he turned and quietly returned to his duties.

The next morning, he bowed to the master and said humbly, "Yesterday I was disrespectful."

"If you understand this much, that's enough," the master replied, sensing something special in the young monk.

On another day, the master pointed to the bright sun in the sky, testing the monk's understanding. In response, the monk simply waved his hand and began to walk away.

"So you reject my teaching!" the master called after him.

The monk turned back and replied, "Master, you point to the sun, I wave my hand. Where is the rejection?"

"One must be mindful in all situations," the master reminded him gently.

Seeing the monk's genuine understanding—shown not through clever words but through simple, direct actions—the master recognized him as a true student of the Way.

~~~~~~~~~~

*Truth is found in the simplest moments—in an offered orange, in a shared glance, in a wave of the hand. What more needs to be said?*

# SOUND OF SLEEP

One drowsy afternoon in the meditation hall, a master was taking a nap. Another teacher entered and, seeing him sleeping, struck the chair sharply with a staff. The master briefly opened his eyes, glanced at the visitor, and peacefully returned to his slumber.

Later, the teacher walked to the front of the hall, where he found the head monk sitting in formal meditation. Looking at the monk's rigid posture, the teacher scolded, "The monk back there is truly meditating while he sleeps, yet here you sit, lost in scattered thoughts."

～～～～～～～

When sleeping is just sleeping, even snores teach dharma. When trying to meditate, even silence is noise.

# MASTER OF STILLNESS

High in the mountains, there lived a Zen master known for his unshakable stillness. For over thirty years, he never left his sanctuary. Though renowned for his enlightenment through meditation, he also deeply studied the scriptures, harmonizing practice with understanding.

One evening, a troubled student approached him with a familiar difficulty.

"Master, when I sit in meditation at night, my thoughts scatter like leaves in the wind. I cannot find a way to calm them. Please teach me."

The master smiled gently and replied:

"When you sit quietly at night and find your thoughts flying about, turn your attention to the thoughts themselves. Ask yourself: Where do these scattered thoughts actually dwell?

"When you search for their dwelling place, you'll find there is none. And if they have no home, how can these scattered thoughts exist?

"Then turn your investigation back on itself: Where is this mind that's doing the investigating?

"You'll discover that the wisdom which observes is essentially empty, and the objects it observes are naturally quiet.

"In true stillness, there is no one being still. In true seeing, there is nothing being seen.

"When both observer and observed dissolve, the mind

rests in natural peace. Don't chase external things, and don't cling to inner stillness. When both paths disappear, your original nature shines forth effortlessly.

"This is the essential path back to your true self."

~~~~~~~~~~~~~~~~~

Like trying to catch your own shadow, the more you chase after a quiet mind, the more it eludes you. When we stop the chase and rest in present awareness, we find that peace was here all along, like a clear sky behind the passing clouds.

# HIDDEN THIEF

In a quiet temple, a master sat in his simple quarters when a young monk approached with a puzzling question.

"Master, what should we do when our poor house is being robbed?"

The master's eyes twinkled as he replied, "We can never completely drive the thief away."

Confused, the monk asked, "But why not?"

"Because the thief is a family member," the master said softly.

"If the thief is family, why would he steal from us?"

"When you're at peace inside, nothing outside can truly trouble you," the master said, pouring tea into two cups.

"What happens when we catch this thief?" the monk persisted.

"Then all disturbance between inside and outside vanishes."

"And what reward do we get for catching the thief?"

"I've never heard of any reward," the master replied with a smile.

"Then isn't our effort wasted?"

"The achievement is real, but we don't hold onto it," the master said, watching the steam rise from his tea.

"Why not hold onto such an achievement?"

The master lifted cup and replied, "Just as a general brings peace to the land but doesn't remain to glory in it."

~~~~~~~~~~~~

The thief we fear is closer than family - it's our own mind creating disturbance between inside and outside.

# STONE IN THE SNOW

In the depths of winter, three young monks were traveling south in search of wisdom. Heavy snow forced them to take shelter at a remote temple.

One evening, as they warmed themselves by the fire, the master of the temple asked, "Where are you heading?"

"We're on a spiritual journey," one of the monks replied.

"And what is the essence of such a journey?"

"I don't know," the monk answered honestly.

"That's the truest answer," the master said with a smile.

Later, their conversation turned to deeper matters. "Are the mountains and rivers separate from you, or one with you?" the master suddenly asked.

"Separate," the monk replied confidently.

The master quietly raised two fingers.

"Ah, then they must be one with me," the monk quickly corrected himself.

The master raised two fingers again and walked away, leaving the monk in confusion.

When the snow cleared and the monks prepared to leave, the master walked them to the gate. Pointing to a large stone in the courtyard, he asked, "You say all realms exist in the mind. Tell me, is this stone inside your mind or outside?"

"Inside my mind," the monk answered confidently.

"Then why would a traveling monk carry such a heavy stone in his mind?"

The monk stood speechless. In that moment, the three monks put down their traveling bags and decided to stay and study with the master.

For a month, the first monk shared his understanding daily, but the master always responded, "That's not the true dharma."

Finally, in despair, the monk admitted, "I have no more words or theories."

The master smiled warmly and said, "The truth is right here, complete in everything."

In that moment, the monk understood. All three eventually found their insight under the master's gentle guidance.

～～～～～～

Outside or inside? One or separate? Every answer is another stone in our mind.

# COLORS OF PURITY

A seeker once approached a master with a question about purity.

"What about something as white as frost or snow—surely that is pure and untainted?"

"That too is contamination," the master replied.

Puzzled, the seeker asked, "Then what is truly pure and untainted?"

"All the colors of the rainbow!" declared the master.

～～～～～～

We search for purity in whiteness, in emptiness, in the absence of color. But perhaps true purity isn't found in what we remove, but in embracing the whole spectrum of existence.

# CIRCLE IN THE AIR

In a quiet monastery, two respected teachers were known for their contrasting teachings. One master often taught, "No beings possess Buddha-nature," while another proclaimed, "All beings possess Buddha-nature." Though both were wise and revered, their opposing teachings stirred debate among their students.

One day, two monks from the second master's temple, confident in their understanding, visited the monastery of the first teacher. They heard the teaching that "no beings possess Buddha-nature" and felt a quiet disdain, believing their own master's view to be superior.

While wandering the monastery grounds, they encountered a senior monk, a disciple of the first master, and condescendingly advised him, "Brother, you must study the dharma diligently. Don't take it lightly!"

The senior monk responded without words. He raised his hands and drew a circle in the air. Then, with a small, deliberate motion, he tossed the circle behind his back. Extending his empty hands toward them, he silently waited, as though asking for something in return.

The two monks stood in bewildered silence.

The senior monk smiled and repeated their earlier advice: "Brothers, you must study the dharma diligently. Don't take it lightly!" Then he turned and walked away.

On their journey home, the two monks walked in silence, each deep in thought. After traveling about thirty miles, one of them stopped suddenly, his face alight with understanding. "Now I see why the teaching says no beings possess Buddha-nature!" Without hesitation, he turned back toward the monastery to continue his study.

The second monk continued walking alone. As he crossed a river, the sound of splashing water awakened something within him. "Ah! The teaching is absolutely true!" He, too, returned to study under the first master.

~~~~~~~~~~~~~~

An empty circle in the air - what can you grasp? What can you possess? To truly understand "no Buddha-nature," first throw away your understanding of Buddha-nature.

# A QUESTION OF DONKEYS

Long ago, a monk returned to his teacher's monastery after years of study with other masters. Upon his arrival, the teacher greeted him with an unusual conversation.

"Why have you come?" the teacher asked.

"To pay my respects to you, Master," the monk replied simply.

"And do you see the master?"

"Yes, I do."

The teacher's eyes twinkled with mischief. "How does the master compare to a donkey?"

Without hesitation, the monk responded, "When I look at you, Master, I don't even see a Buddha."

"Oh?" the teacher leaned forward. "If not a Buddha, what do you see?"

The monk smiled gently. "If I compared you to anything at all, how would that be different from comparing you to a donkey?"

The teacher burst into delighted laughter. "In twenty years of testing students, no one has seen so clearly! You have transcended both the sacred and the ordinary. You have stripped away all concepts to reveal the bare truth."

From that day forward, whenever the teacher spoke of the monk to others, he would say with deep appreciation, "This one is Buddha in the flesh."

The monk later established his own temple on a distant mountain, where he taught countless students

with the same directness that had shaped his own understanding.

~~~~~~~~~~~~~~~

Labels are cages, even golden ones. Freedom lies in seeing
without naming or comparing.

# DHARMA IN A PINCH

A nun traveled far to visit a renowned master, seeking the deepest truth of the Buddhist teachings.

"What is the most intimate truth of Buddha's dharma?" she asked earnestly.

Without a word, the master reached out and pinched her arm.

The nun recoiled, startled. "Master, I see you still have that kind of desire in you," she said disapprovingly.

The master replied calmly, "No—it is you who still has that kind of thinking in you."

~~~~~~~~~~

A pinch on the arm—so simple, so direct. Yet we wrap it in layers of judgment, interpretation, and assumption. The mirror of our minds reflects not the world as it is, but our own thoughts dancing in the glass.

# MOUNTAIN'S SECRET

A monk once approached a master with a question that had been weighing on his mind.

"Master," he asked, "in the steep cliffs and remote peaks, can the Buddha's teachings still be found?"

The master looked at him with gentle eyes and replied, "Tell me first—what do you call 'steep cliffs and remote peaks'?"

The monk stood silent, suddenly seeing mountains everywhere.

~~~~~~~~~~~~~~~~

Mountains are not just where rocks touch the sky. In the falling leaf, in the marketplace crowd, in the morning tea—every place holds the same vast height. We only need to stop drawing lines between here and there.

# GOOSE IN THE BOTTLE

A man came to a master with a riddle.

"There is a goose in a bottle," he said. "The goose has grown too large to get out through the bottle's neck. Now, without breaking the bottle or harming the goose, how do you get the goose out?"

The master suddenly called out, "Hey!"

Startled, the man instinctively responded, "Yes?"

"There! The goose is out!" declared the master.

In that instant, the man's understanding bloomed like a flower in spring.

~~~~~~~~~

Sometimes we trap ourselves in bottles of our own making—questions that have no answers, problems that exist only in thought. The goose was never really stuck; it was our mind that needed freeing.

# WRONG READING, RIGHT

# AWAKENING

One autumn evening, a master sat reading the
Śūraṅgama Sutra by candlelight. The sacred lines before
him were meant to be read:

"When knowledge gives rise to knowledge, it becomes
the root of ignorance.

When knowledge perceives no knowledge, this is
nirvana itself."

But in the flickering light, the master misread the
passage, breaking the lines differently:

"When knowledge arises,

Knowledge becomes the root of ignorance.

When knowledge ceases,

Seeing this is nirvana itself."

In that moment of "mistaken" reading, like a moon-
beam piercing through clouds, understanding flooded his
mind. When others later pointed out the error, he smiled
gently and said, "This is where I found my awakening. I
wouldn't change it for anything in the world."

Years later, as spring arrived in his final year, he
composed a verse:

"This truth was not carried from mountain peaks,

Nor passed down from the Buddha's sacred seat.

All ancient sages found it just this way—

I haven't crafted something new today."

Then, with the same clarity that marked his awakening, he ordered a coffin brought to his meditation hall. After bathing and changing into fresh robes, he calmly climbed in and asked for the lid to be closed. Three days later, his disciples opened the coffin to find him resting peacefully on his right side. As their grief filled the air, he suddenly sat up and spoke one final teaching:

"Whoever opens this coffin again is no longer my student."

Then, without another word, he lay back down, departing like autumn leaves falling in perfect stillness.

~~~~~~~~~~

*Sometimes our "mistakes" are the very gates of understanding. Like a bird accidentally flying through an open window.*

# MENDER OF EMPTY SPACE

In a small village, there lived a peculiar craftsman known simply as "the Mender." He spent his days repairing broken chairs, polishing mirrors, and fixing whatever people brought to him. Though humble in his trade, he carried the heart of a seeker.

One day, the mender visited a renowned master. The master asked him, "Are you the one they call the Mender?"

"I wouldn't dare claim so," the mender replied humbly.

"Can you mend empty space?" the master asked, his eyes sharp.

"Please break it first, Master," the mender replied with a wry smile.

Without hesitation, the master lifted his staff and struck the mender.

Confused and hurt, the mender protested, "Master, why do you strike me without cause?"

"Later, a teacher with more words will help you understand," the master replied cryptically.

Still puzzled, the mender traveled to meet another master and recounted his experience.

"Why did the first master strike you?" the second master asked.

"I don't know what I did wrong," the mender admitted.

The second master's eyes gleamed as he said, "You

can't even handle this single crack!"

In that moment, the mender's confusion dissolved like mist. He bowed deeply in gratitude.

The second master added with a smile, "Now, mend this crack."

~~~~~~~~~~

Before the staff falls, empty space is unbroken. After the strike, who is there to mend? The real crack appears when we think something needs fixing.

# DANCING WITH CATTLE

One quiet afternoon, a master and a disciple were tending to the monastery's cattle. The herd grazed peacefully on the hillside, their bells tinkling softly in the mountain breeze.

Pointing to the grazing herd, the master asked, "Are there any bodhisattvas among these cattle?"

"Yes," the disciple replied without hesitation.

"Show me," said the master, "which one is a bodhisattva?"

The disciple gazed at the peaceful herd for a moment, then turned to his teacher with a gentle smile. "Master, perhaps you could show me which one isn't a bodhisattva?"

The master laughed, his laughter blending with the sound of cow bells in the mountain air.

~~~~~~~~~~~~

Like sunlight falling equally on every blade of grass, truth makes no distinction between this cow or that.

# FLOWER IN THE INCENSE BURNER

One quiet morning, a senior monk visited a master at a forest temple. In his hand, he carried a fresh flower. Without a word, he walked once around the master's meditation platform, then casually placed the flower in the incense burner behind his back.

"Master," he asked, "what do you make of this?"

The master offered several interpretations, each more profound than the last, but none seemed to capture the true meaning. For two months, the question lingered in his mind like morning mist.

Finally, he invited the senior monk to explain the significance of his action that day.

The senior monk replied simply, "I just put a flower in the incense burner. Why did you make such a mystery of it?"

～～～～～～

We search for hidden meanings in every shadow, turning simple moments into puzzles that need solving. Meanwhile, the flower sits quietly in the burner, asking nothing, explaining nothing.

# ANCIENT BUDDHA IN THE KITCHEN

A group of wandering monks once traveled great distances to study under a renowned master. Upon their arrival, the master greeted them harshly:

"What are you wanderers doing here? Do you think I have spare rice to feed idle mouths?"

When they stood their ground, the master threw water on them. When that didn't drive them away, he scattered ashes over their heads. Most of the monks stormed off in anger, but two of them remained seated, unmoved.

"Why do you stay when others have left?" the master demanded.

"We've traveled a thousand miles seeking your wisdom," one of the monks replied calmly. "How could a splash of water or a handful of ash turn us away?"

Seeing their sincerity, the master allowed them to stay and appointed one of them as the temple cook.

Life at the monastery was austere. One day, while the master was away, the cook gave in to the monks' pleas and prepared a rich, nourishing porridge. When the master returned and discovered this, he confiscated the cook's robes and bowls to pay for the "stolen" provisions and expelled him from the monastery.

But the cook didn't leave. Instead, he found shelter in

a corridor down the mountain and continued climbing up daily to hear the master's teachings. When discovered months later, he was scolded again for "stealing" lodging and forced to beg in town to repay his debt.

Through it all, the cook's respect for the master only deepened.

Finally, after observing the cook's quiet perseverance, the master gathered the monks and announced: "There is an ancient Buddha among us."

"Who?" the monks asked, astonished.

The master replied, "The cook is truly an ancient Buddha."

~~~~~~~~~~

The ancient Buddha wasn't hiding in the kitchen - he was revealed through endless patience and unwavering devotion.

# WOOD CARRIER'S

# ENLIGHTENMENT

One day, a monk joined his brothers in the daily labor, carrying firewood across the temple grounds. As he worked, the master approached him.

"Are you carrying wood today?" the master asked.

"Yes," the monk replied simply.

"There's an old question," the master said. "'Does the person carry the wood, or does the wood carry the person?' What do you make of this?"

The monk stood silent, the wood resting in his arms.

The master continued, "It's like learning calligraphy. A beginner focuses on each stroke, trying to copy perfectly. Their writing is either skilled or clumsy because they haven't forgotten the rules. True mastery comes when the brush forgets the hand, the hand forgets the mind, and the mind forgets itself."

After a moment of reflection, the monk replied, "As the ancient master said, 'To cling to action is delusion, to grasp understanding is not enlightenment.'"

"Are those words medicine or sickness?" the master challenged.

"Medicine," the monk answered confidently.

"Ah, but you're mistaking the sickness for the cure!"

The monk protested, "When action fits like a lid on a box, when reason flows straight as an arrow—what more could there be?"

The master shook his head. "Even perfect harmony between action and reason is still just action and reason. The true way lies beyond what intellect can grasp. As Buddha said, 'Reason blocks true seeing, and action perpetuates the cycle of birth and death.'"

Suddenly, the monk understood. "Then how should one proceed?"

"As long as you stay within conventional boundaries, how can you break free?"

The monk sighed in realization. "The moment words leave our lips, meaning gets trapped in thought. These are all dead ends, not the living path."

~~~~~~~~~

Sometimes we carry the wood, and sometimes the wood carries us. Between these two truths lies a space where the brush, the hand, and the mind become one flowing river. In that space, even our most perfect understanding becomes another weight to put down.

# SIX ONES

A master carved six wooden dice. Strangely, on each face of every die, he inscribed only a single dot.

Whenever a monk visited seeking wisdom, the master would roll all six dice across the floor. The dots stared up like tiny eyes in the silence.

"Do you understand?" he would ask.

If the monk hesitated even for a breath, the master would raise his staff and chase him away.

---

When every face shows One, what is there to calculate? The master's staff waits for those who look twice at what's perfectly clear the first time.

# SLEEPING SAGE

A monk arrived at a monastery and spent his days doing nothing but sleeping in the meditation hall. He showed no interest in formal practice or questioning, simply curling up and drifting off while others meditated.

The hall monitor, deeply disturbed by this behavior, scolded him repeatedly, but the monk paid no attention and continued his peaceful slumber.

Finally, the frustrated monitor went to the master and reported, "There's a monk here who does nothing but sleep all day. We must enforce the rules!"

"Who is it?" asked the master.

"Senior Monk Ch'ing," replied the hall monitor.

"Let me look into this myself," said the master thoughtfully.

Taking his staff, the master went to the meditation hall and found the monk sound asleep. He rapped on the platform sharply and said, "We don't offer free meals here for monks to sleep away the day!"

The monk opened his eyes lazily. "What would you have me do, Master?"

"Why don't you practice meditation like the others?"

The monk stretched and replied, "Fine food holds no appeal to one who is already full."

"Many here disapprove of your behavior," the master pressed.

The monk shrugged. "If they approved, what good

would that do?"

Curious, the master asked, "Who was your previous teacher?"

"Master Fu-shan," the monk replied.

At this, the master burst into laughter. "Ah! That explains your stubborn wisdom!"

The two exchanged knowing smiles and clasped hands. From that day forward, the monk's reputation spread far and wide.

~~~~~~~~~~~~

What looks like laziness to some eyes might be the deepest practice to others. Who can judge another's path?

# GARDEN OF NO SHADOWS

In a quiet mountain monastery, the head gardener was hard at work under the guidance of the master. One day, after finishing his tasks, the gardener stood before the master to report.

"What have you been doing today?" the master asked.

"Planting vegetables," the gardener replied matter-of-factly.

"If the entire universe is Buddha's body, where do you find space to plant?" the master challenged.

With a slight smile, the gardener answered, "The golden hoe never disturbs the soil, yet sacred sprouts grow everywhere."

The master nodded in approval.

On another day, the master visited the garden and called out, "Gardener!"

"Yes, Master?"

"Plant a shadowless tree for future generations to see," the master instructed.

The gardener tilted his head thoughtfully. "If it casts no shadow, how can it be planted?"

"Leave aside whether it can be planted," the master replied. "Have you ever seen its branches and leaves?"

"Never," the gardener admitted.

"If you've never seen them, how do you know it cannot be planted?"

"Precisely because I've never seen them, I know it cannot be planted," the gardener replied with a calm smile.

The master's face lit up. "Indeed! Indeed!"

Years later, as the master lay on his deathbed, he called for the gardener one last time.

"After the sun sets behind the western mountains, don't settle for comfort," the master whispered.

The gardener replied, "Snow covers the golden sandalwood, yet its sacred branches remain forever in spring."

~~~~~~~~~~

In the garden of no-mind, shadowless trees grow naturally, and golden hoes leave no trace.

# PORTRAIT'S SECRET

At a mountain monastery, old Zen master once inscribed a portrait of himself with these words:
"Rain washes the tender pink of peach buds,
Wind stirs the delicate green of willow threads.
Among white clouds, strange rocks emerge,
In clear waters, ancient trees reflect.
Ah, who are you?"

Years later, a monk visited the monastery where the portrait hung. Looking at it together with the current master of the monastery, the visiting monk admired the verse.

The current master smiled and said, "Now I understand why he is considered truly enlightened."

Puzzled, the visiting monk asked, "How can you tell, just from these simple words about scenery, that he is enlightened?"

"For many years," the current master replied, "people have mistaken mere descriptions of nature for true understanding. But look deeper - what do you see beyond the words?"

In that moment, the visiting monk's eyes brightened with sudden insight. "Ah, so that's it!"

"What do you see?" the master pressed.

"Spring births, summer grows, autumn harvests, winter stores," the monk answered.

The master nodded with approval. "Now guard this

understanding well."

The monk bowed deeply in gratitude.

~~~~~~~~~~~~~~~~

The peach blossoms and willow threads are not mere scenery—
they are the face we wore before we were born, the voice that
speaks without sound. Who indeed are you, behind these eyes
that see the rain?

# FIRE TONGS

One day, a master held up his walking stick during a teaching and proclaimed to the assembly:

"If you have a staff, I'll give you one. If you don't have a staff, I'll take it away."

With that, he set the staff down and left, leaving the monks to ponder his words.

One practitioner struggled with this koan for years, turning it over and over in his mind without finding clarity. One winter evening, he stood beside another master, who was warming himself by the fire.

Suddenly, the master asked, "Tell me about the walking stick koan."

As the practitioner opened his mouth to speak, the master snatched the fire tongs and struck him.

In that instant, the practitioner's understanding burst open, as sudden and vivid as sparks flying from the fire.

Years later, when he became a teacher himself, he addressed his assembly with these words:

"Height is not found at the summit,
Wealth is not found in abundance.
Joy is not found in heaven,
Suffering is not found in hell."

After a long pause, he added:

"We may know faces all over the world,
But how many truly know our heart?"

~~~~~~~~~~~~~~~~~

The mind carries sticks for years, but the body knows in one strike.

# MUTE'S HONEY

At a quiet mountain monastery, a monk approached the master with a question that had been burning in his heart.

"What is it like," the monk asked, "when one knows the Way but cannot express it?"

The master replied, "Like a mute person tasting honey."

The monk pressed further. "And what of those who can speak of the Way but don't truly know it?"

"Like a parrot calling out names," the master responded.

The monk bowed deeply, convinced he had grasped the lesson.

But the master scolded him sharply, "Ah, you're just another message carrier!"

~~~~~~~~~~

The sweetest honey leaves no trace on the tongue, and the truest word has never been spoken. Between the mute's knowing smile and the parrot's empty chatter lies a taste that no messenger can deliver.

# SNOWY DIALOGUE

One winter afternoon, two masters sat together, discussing how great teachers of the past had come to their awakening. As they spoke, snow began to fall, blanketing the earth in white stillness.

Pointing to the snow-covered ground, one master asked, "Can this be swept away with a bamboo broom?"

"No," the other replied. "But when the sky clears and the sun emerges, when the clouds disperse and the snow melts, revealing the contrast of dark and light—what then remains to be swept? One who truly understands moves through all words and phrases like a blade through bamboo—what need is there for deliberation?"

Later, to test this understanding further, the first master sent a monk to ask the other about the "three barriers" of an ancient teacher.

The response thundered like a clap of lightning: "Why concern yourself with matters from the distant past?"

When the first master heard of this reply, he nodded in approval. From that day, the other master's reputation spread far and wide, carried on the winds of the mountains.

~~~~~~~~~~~~~~~~

*Snow falls without asking where it will land, and melts without leaving a trace. In the space between falling and melting, what broom could sweep away the truth that was never there?*

# ILLITERATE SAGE

In a quiet monastery, there lived a humble monk who could neither read nor write. Despite his simple appearance and lack of education, his heart burned with a desire to understand the teachings. While others studied texts and debated concepts, he devoted himself to practice under a skilled master.

His fellow monks, however, often mocked him for his awkward demeanor and ignorance. Their jeers fell from him as easily as morning dew slips from a lotus leaf.

One day, the monk asked his peers earnestly, "What is Zen?"

Seeking to mock him further, they replied, "Go ask the singing cicada!"

Not understanding the insult, the monk turned to the wall in deep contemplation. Day and night, he sat without moving, his body growing thin as a reed in winter.

Months passed in silence. One day, while walking through the temple courtyard, he stumbled and fell. In that moment of meeting the earth, something broke open within him. Enlightenment burst forth, clear and undeniable.

Unable to write, he asked a novice to inscribe his realization on the temple wall:

"This tumble, this fall,
Worth more than mountains of gold.
Hat on my head, bundle at my waist,

Pure wind and bright moon hanging from my staff."
Without another word, the monk left the temple.

When the master heard of this, his face lit up with joy. "Such is true practice!" he exclaimed, and sent monks to find the awakened one. But like morning mist, he had vanished without a trace.

～～～～～～～～～

Sometimes wisdom doesn't come through books but through stumbling. It doesn't arise from clever words but from graceless falls. The brightest moon needs no letters to write its light across the evening sky.

# YESTERDAY'S RAIN, TODAY'S SUN

One day, a scholar approached a Zen master with a challenge in his voice. "Why do Zen teachings seem to lack foundation?" he asked, confident in his vast knowledge of scripture.

The master responded with a gentle question of his own: "What scriptures have you studied?"

"I have a general understanding of various sutras," the scholar replied proudly, "and I'm particularly well-versed in the Hundred Dharmas."

The master smiled and asked, "Tell me then, under which dharma would you classify yesterday's rain and today's sunshine?"

The scholar stood silent, his knowledge suddenly useless before the simplicity of the question.

The master playfully tapped him with a back scratcher and said, "Perhaps you shouldn't be so quick to dismiss Zen teachings!"

Frustrated, the scholar's face reddened, and he demanded, "Well then, which dharma does contain yesterday's rain and today's sunshine?"

"It falls under the twenty-fourth division," the master replied calmly, "the category of phenomena that cannot be categorized."

In that moment, the scholar's understanding broke

open, like clouds parting after rain. He bowed deeply in gratitude.

~~~~~~~~~~~~~~~~~~

Rain falls, sun shines, each perfect in its moment. How funny that we try to catch the wind in nets of words, when even yesterday's weather slips through our finest categories like water through cupped hands.

# WATCH THE FIRE!

One winter day, a government official and devoted student sat with a Zen master around a brazier, warming themselves by its glow.

"Master," the student said, "let's set aside all the old stories and koans. Give me one direct teaching, right here and now."

The master suddenly bowed formally, then shouted with urgent intensity: "Watch the fire!"

Startled, the student frantically patted his robes, thinking they had caught fire. In that moment of alarm, something burst open within him, like a flame breaking through paper. He bowed deeply, joy spreading across his face.

"Ah! How clear! The Buddha's teaching is really nothing special at all!"

"Now drop that too!" the master thundered.

"Yes, yes!" the student responded, bowing again and again.

~~~~~~~~~~

Sometimes it takes a shout to wake us to the simple warmth that's always been there, waiting.

# IMAGINARY DOG

A master lived in solitude on a remote mountain, dwelling in a simple thatched hut. When the locals gifted him a temple, he hung an unusual sign at its gate:

"Beware! In this temple dwells a dog:

Above, it takes your head.

In the middle, it takes your heart.

Below, it takes your feet.

Hesitate, and your life is forfeit."

One day, two monks from a distant monastery came to visit. As they lifted the curtain at the temple's gate, the master suddenly shouted:

"Watch out for the dog!"

Startled, the monks spun around, searching for the fearsome beast. But as they looked, the master quietly returned to his quarters, leaving them to their confusion.

~~~~~~~~~~

Sometimes the fiercest guard dog is the one we create in our own minds. While we search the shadows for imaginary teeth, the teacher has already walked away.

# THREE PHRASES

A master posted a notice outside the attendants'
quarters:

"East Mountain has three phrases.

Speak them correctly, and you may stay."

Monks traveled from far and wide to try their luck,
each hoping to decode the mysterious phrases. They studied ancient texts, pondered deeply, and offered countless
answers, but none succeeded.

One day, a travel-worn monk appeared at the master's
door. With a sleeping mat rolled under his arm, he bowed
and said simply:

"I cannot speak the phrases. I only wish to stay."

The master's face lit up with joy. He immediately
called the head monk and had the traveler given the
brightest room in the monastery, where the morning light
first touched the floor.

~~~~~~~~~~

*The wisest answer is to admit we don't have one. In the space
between knowing and not knowing, truth finds its own way
home—like sunlight through an open window.*

# POETRY TRAP

A renowned monk visited a provincial governor who had long admired his wisdom. The governor offered him lodging for the winter and sought his teachings daily. Word of the monk's presence quickly spread, and soon another official requested poems for his garden pavilion through the governor.

"I carry not a single word in my mind," the monk said, declining several times. But as the requests persisted, the governor, hoping to inspire him, placed collections of classical poetry before him.

Reluctantly, the monk opened one volume. Suddenly, verses began flowing like a spring flood—unstoppable. By the time the governor returned from a brief errand, over thirty poems had poured onto paper.

In that moment, the monk caught himself: "Ah, this is the trap of literary habit!" He stopped writing, shared only one poem, and set the rest aside. But the verses continued surging through his mind. All the poetry and literature he had ever read now filled the void like storm clouds, threatening to burst. Even with countless mouths, he could not have spoken it all.

Recognizing this challenge to his practice, the monk sat in meditation and closed his door. When servants knocked, he gave no answer. Worried, they eventually climbed through a window, only to find him seated motionless as a wooden statue, unresponsive to calls or movement.

The governor struck a bell several times before the monk slowly emerged from his deep meditation. "Master," the governor said, "you've been sitting here for five days!"

After this experience, the monk's memories of his years of wandering and practice seemed like distant dreams. The flood of verses that had filled his mind dispersed like clouds after rain, leaving the sky pristinely empty. His heart became as clear as still water, finding joy in ultimate simplicity.

Later, he said:

"In perfect stillness, light penetrates all.

In silent illumination, emptiness holds everything.

Looking back at the world of forms, all appears as dreams."

Like a lake that has forgotten its ripples, the clearest mind holds nothing, reflects everything.

~~~~~~~~~~~

When the last poem dissolves, when the final word fades, what remains is clearer than any verse could capture.

# MOUNTAIN PATH

At the foot of a great mountain lived an old woman known for giving directions to traveling monks. One day, a pilgrim approached her and asked, "Which way leads to the mountain?"

"Straight ahead," she replied. But as the monk walked away, she muttered under her breath, "Another good monk goes just like that."

Word of her strange remark reached a renowned master. Intrigued, he decided to investigate for himself. The next day, he visited the old woman.

"Which way to the mountain's back path?" he asked.

"Straight ahead," she answered. Just as before, as he walked away, she murmured, "Another good monk goes just like that."

Returning to his temple, the master smiled and told his disciples, "That old woman by the mountain—she sees right through us all."

~~~~~~~~~~

The path is always straight ahead, yet we keep searching for hidden meanings in the signpost rather than in our own steps.

# MASTER OF TIME

A young monk approached an old master with a question that had long troubled him. "How should one direct the mind throughout the twelve hours of the day?"

The master looked up from his simple meal and smiled. "You let the hours use you," he said, "while I use the hours themselves."

Seeing the monk's confusion, the master continued: "Listen well. If you have something to discuss, let us discuss it. If not, go sit quietly and contemplate. In all my years, I've simply let each activity be what it is—eating when eating, walking when walking. I've never tried to maintain any special state of mind."

Pausing to sip his tea, he added, "If you live differently, you're wandering far from the path."

~~~~~~~~~

Time flows like a river—we can either be swept along by its current, always watching the hours, or we can wade in its waters, letting each moment simply be.

# BAMBOO SIEVE MAKERS

In a small market town, a father and daughter made their living crafting bamboo sieves. They lived simply, weaving wisdom into their daily lives as naturally as they wove bamboo strips. Their humble cottage often rang with gentle laughter as they worked and shared insights.

One day, the father tested his daughter. "The ancient ones spoke of seeing the master's mind in every blade of grass. What do you make of this?"

The daughter teased, "Oh, father, why speak in such riddles?"

"Then how would you say it?" he asked.

She replied simply, "Every blade of grass shows the master's mind."

The father smiled, seeing the depth of her understanding.

Another time, as they crossed a bridge, the father stumbled and fell. Instead of helping him up, the daughter fell down beside him.

"What are you doing?" he asked.

"I saw you fall, so I'm helping you," she replied with a twinkle in her eye.

When the father's time grew near, he asked his daughter to watch the sun and tell him when it reached its peak. She soon returned, announcing, "The sun is at its peak, but strangely, there's an eclipse!"

As the father stepped outside to look, she quietly sat

on his meditation cushion and departed this world with a peaceful smile. Finding her, the father chuckled, "Ah, my clever daughter, always one step ahead!"

He stayed for seven more days to arrange her funeral. When his own time came, resting against a friend's knee, he shared his final teaching: "May all that exists become empty, but do not make real that which does not exist. Live well—all things in this world are like echoes and shadows."

With these words, he too departed.

~~~~~~~~~~~

Like bamboo sieves separating clear water from sediment, our lives filter the essential from the superficial. Wisdom flourishes in the quiet rhythm of daily life, between the weaving of bamboo strips and ordinary conversation.

# BURNING STATUE

On a bitter winter night, when snow blanketed the temple grounds and the cold cut through to the bone, a master found shelter in a small temple. As the temperature dropped further, he did something unexpected—he took a wooden Buddha statue from the shrine and set it ablaze in the hearth.

The temple keeper, hearing the crackle of flames, rushed over in horror. "How dare you burn our sacred Buddha statue!"

The master calmly stirred the ashes with his staff and replied, "I'm searching for the sacred relics."

"What relics? This is just a wooden statue!" the keeper exclaimed.

"Ah," said the master, still warming his hands by the fire, "if there are no relics, then we should fetch another statue to keep warm."

The firelight danced on the walls as the keeper stood frozen, his long-held beliefs crumbling like the wooden statue. In that moment, he glimpsed the truth that lay beyond form and appearance.

~~~~~~~~~~~~~~~

A wooden Buddha sits silently in the hall, neither sacred nor profane. What transforms in the fire is not the statue, but our own clinging to empty forms.

# CANDLE

In the deep stillness of night, the meditation hall was silent. A young monk had been standing quietly beside his master for many hours. As the night grew late, the master turned to him and said, "You should take rest now."

The monk bowed and stepped outside. After a moment, he returned and whispered, "Master, it is dark outside."

The master lit a single candle, its warm glow casting soft shadows on the walls. Just as the monk reached for it, the master blew out the flame.

In that sudden darkness, where even shadows disappeared, something shifted. The young monk stood motionless, his breath catching in the stillness. Then, without a word, he bowed—not out of courtesy, but from a place of genuine understanding.

The master smiled silently in the dark.

Years later, when asked about that night, the monk would only say, "Some things can be seen only when there is nothing to see."

~~~~~~~~~~~~~~~~

A candle casts both light and shadow. But in the depth of night, when no flame burns, the eyes adjust, and the world reveals itself in ways that light could never show. Perhaps what we think illuminates our path sometimes casts the deepest shadows.

# SIMPLE WAY

A seeker approached a master, eager to uncover the secret of his practice.

"How do you cultivate your mind?" the seeker asked.

The master replied simply, "When hungry, I eat. When tired, I sleep."

The seeker was puzzled. "But everyone does that! Are they all practicing as you do?"

The master's eyes twinkled. "No," he said. "When they eat, their minds wander through a hundred desires. When they sleep, their thoughts race through a thousand concerns. They are never truly here."

~~~~~~~~~~~~~~

We search for profound truths in distant mountains while missing the wisdom in our bowl of rice. The deepest practice isn't found in adding something special, but in removing what separates us from this moment—this breath, this bite, this rest.

# HEART'S MIRROR

In a valley known for its ever-changing weather, a young monk sat with his master beneath a pine tree, watching clouds gather and disperse over the mountain peaks.

"Master," the monk sighed, "why must winter be so harsh? Why must summer burn so fiercely? Only spring and autumn bring true beauty."

The master picked up a fallen leaf, its edges touched by frost.

"Tell me," he said, "does the sky choose to bring rain? Does the wind decide to be gentle or strong? When snow falls, does it select where to land?"

The monk remained silent.

"Nature simply is," the master continued, holding up the leaf. "It is our heart that paints it beautiful or ugly. The seasons flow without preference—only we divide them into what we love and what we reject."

The monk watched as the master released the leaf, letting it dance away on the wind.

~~~~~~~~~~

A mirror doesn't judge what it reflects. The mountains don't prefer spring's flowers to winter's snow. Wisdom lies not in seeking perfect seasons, but in discovering why we paint some moments gold and others gray.

# BEYOND FORMALITIES

An eager seeker traveled far to meet a great master. Upon arriving at the temple, he marched straight to the meditation hall, his staff jingling and water bottle swaying. Without bowing, he walked around the master three times.

The master looked up. "A monk should observe three thousand protocols and eighty thousand subtle practices. Where do you come from, showing such pride?"

The seeker replied instantly, "Life and death are pressing matters. Time waits for no one."

The master's eyes softened. "Why seek in such haste? Your true nature was never born and exists beyond time itself."

"Yes," the seeker answered. "What is truly real was never born, and knows no hurry."

The master smiled. "Just so, just so."

~~~~~~~~~~

We rush through life chasing time, yet what we truly are remains forever still, like the depths of the ocean untouched by waves. True urgency lies not in racing against time, but in awakening to what time cannot touch.

# WITHOUT WORDS

A master sat before his disciples in the meditation hall. Morning light filtered through the paper windows, and dust motes danced in the silent air.

"Speak," the master challenged, "but without using your throat or lips."

One monk stepped forward and said, "Master, I will not speak. Please, you show us instead."

The master nodded approvingly. "I dare not demonstrate," he replied, "for if I created a way to show it, future generations would be like those who stare at the finger pointing to the moon, never seeing the moon itself."

~~~~~~~~~~~~~~~~

*Words are boats we use to cross rivers of meaning. But once we reach the other shore, the boat is no longer needed. How do you pass on what cannot be spoken? Like trying to catch mist in a jar, any method becomes another barrier.*

# ONE LETTER

A master once asked his young disciple, "How many sutras do you read each day?"

"Seven or eight volumes, sometimes even ten," the disciple replied proudly.

"Then you don't know how to read sutras," the master said simply.

Puzzled, the disciple asked, "Master, how many do you read each day?"

The master's eyes twinkled. "I read just one letter each day."

~~~~~~~~~~~~

Reading is not about how many pages we turn, but about how deeply we let each word turn us.

# WANDERER

In the golden light of evening, a young monk arrived at a mountain temple. The old master sat on a wooden platform, watching the newcomer approach.

"Where do you come from?" the master asked.

"Nowhere," replied the young monk.

"Then why not return?" the master inquired.

"There is nowhere to return to."

The master shook his head gently. "Your mind wanders too far in emptiness."

The young monk smiled. "Only my feet wander on the path."

~~~~~~~~

We speak of coming and going, of here and there, while clouds drift past, neither arriving nor departing. All journeys are like this—footprints in the morning dew, vanishing even as they form.

# TWO TRUTHS

A merchant visited a Zen master in his humble temple.

"Master, tell me—are heaven and hell real? Are the Three Treasures of Buddha, Dharma, and Sangha truly real?"

To each question, the master calmly replied, "Yes, they are."

The merchant frowned. "But this can't be right. I visited another master on a distant mountain, and he told me there is nothing—everything is empty."

The master smiled and asked, "Do you have a wife?"

"Yes, I do," the merchant replied.

"And does the other master have a wife?"

"No, he doesn't," the merchant admitted.

"Ah," the master nodded. "He lives free of attachments, so for him, all is empty. You live in the world of family and commerce, so for you, things exist. Each answer is true to its way of life."

~~~~~~~~~~~~~~~~

*A river flows differently in the mountains and on the plains, yet it is the same water reaching toward the sea. Some walk the path of form, others the path of emptiness—but both streams flow to the same ocean.*

# LOCK WITHOUT A DOOR

In a remote mountain temple, a master devised a peculiar test for those who sought wisdom. On one wall, he painted a perfect circle with the following inscription:

"Paint the inside without darkening it,

Paint the outside without disturbing its whiteness.

If you can leave your mark without changing either space,

Your path to enlightenment is clear.

If not, turn back in shame."

To add to the challenge, the master hung a lock at the entrance to his chamber. Beside it, he wrote:

"This ancient lock has been passed down

Through countless generations.

Only wisdom serves as its key.

If you cannot unlock what cannot be locked,

No need to seek me."

Day after day, seekers came. Some brought brushes, trying in vain to mark the circle without leaving a trace. Others stood before the lock, puzzled, searching for a key to what was already open.

~~~~~~~~~

We search for doors that were never closed and draw lines between spaces that were never separate. The true key lies in seeing there was never a lock, and the perfect circle was already complete before the first stroke of paint.

# BURNED EYEBROWS

In a mountain temple, the master assigned a young monk to be the fire keeper, responsible for maintaining the kitchen fires and preparing meals for the monastery.

One day, as the young monk carried firewood on his back, the master encountered him and asked, "What are you doing with those thorns?"

"This is firewood," the monk replied simply.

The master burst into laughter and walked away, leaving the monk bewildered.

The young monk put down his load and asked, "Master, what is the meaning behind your question that I failed to grasp?"

The master remained silent and departed, leaving only the echo of his laughter.

This exchange sparked an intense questioning in the young monk's mind. Day and night, he pondered the master's mysterious words while continuing his duties in the kitchen. So absorbed was he in this contemplation that one day, while tending the fire, he didn't notice the flames creeping too close until they singed half his eyebrows.

The sudden sharp pain jolted him to awareness. He rushed to find a mirror, and in that moment of seeing his scorched reflection, understanding struck like lightning. He composed a verse:

"The monk carrying wood calls them merely sticks,
While flames kiss eyebrows with burning tricks.

In the mirror, the ancestors' truth shines clear,
One glance reveals what was always here."
When he showed this verse to the master, the master raised his staff to strike. The young monk caught the staff mid-air, saying, "This six-foot pole has gathered dust for years, yet today it wants to dance again."

The master laughed heartily.

The young monk then offered another verse:
"Where the staff strikes, marks may show,
In laughter, hidden blades may flow.
Only the truly awakened see,
Life in what seems to kill the slow."

The master nodded in approval, recognizing the young monk's awakening as genuine and complete.

～～～～～～～

Sometimes we must lose our eyebrows to find our true face.

# SILENT DANCE OF TWO MOUNTAINS

A wandering monk climbed a remote mountain and came upon a cave where a hermit lived. The hermit, his face weathered by years of solitude, sat in perfect stillness, showing no sign of acknowledging the visitor.

The monk bowed. No response. He tried to speak. Still silence.

Understanding dawned on the monk. He quietly sat down nearby, mirroring the hermit's stillness. When the hermit made tea, he took only one cup. The monk found another cup and drank without a word. When the hermit prepared food, he set out one bowl. The monk found another and ate quietly. At night, when the hermit walked in meditation outside the cave, the monk walked too, each keeping to their own path under the stars.

For seven days, they lived this way—cooking, eating, walking, sitting—all in complete silence. No words, no gestures, just the rhythm of two lives moving in harmony.

On the eighth day, the hermit finally spoke: "Where do you come from?"

"From the south," the monk replied.

"Why are you here?"

"To meet you."

The hermit smiled. "As you see, I am nothing special."

"I saw that the moment I arrived," the monk said.

Laughing softly, the hermit replied, "For thirty years, I've lived here. Today, I finally meet someone who truly understands the way of silence."

They continued living together in the cave. One night, while walking in meditation, the monk experienced a profound awakening. Thunder crashed in his mind, and for a moment, all existence disappeared into emptiness. When he returned to the cave, elated, he shared this experience with the hermit.

The hermit replied gently, "Such experiences come and go like clouds in the sky. I've seen many such moments in my years here. Don't mistake the spectacular for the essential—the truest wisdom is in simply being, just as you are."

~~~~~~~~~~

Two streams merge without a sound, each bringing its own silence to the river. Sometimes the truest companions are those who share our silence.